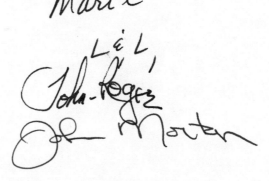

To Bruce &
Marie

L & L,
John-Roger

John Morton

LOVING EACH DAY

Moms & Dads

An Inspirational Guide
and Working Journal for Parents
to Enrich the Spirit within

Books by the Author

A Consciousness of Wealth
Awakening Into Light
Baraka
Blessings of Light
Buddha Consciousness
Divine Essence
Dream Voyages
Drugs
Dynamics of the Lower Self
Forgiveness: The Key to the Kingdom
God Is Your Partner
Inner Worlds of Meditation
Loving...Each Day
Manual on Using the Light
Passage Into Spirit
Possessions, Projections & Entities
Psychic Protection
Q & A Journal from the Heart
Relationships – Love, Marriage and Spirit
Sex, Spirit & You
Spiritual Warrior: The Art of Spiritual Living

BOOKS BY THE AUTHOR

The Christ Within & The Disciples of Christ
with the Cosmic Christ Calendar
The Consciousness of Soul
The Journey of a Soul
The Path to Mastership
The Power Within You
The Signs of the Times
The Sound Current
The Spiritual Family
The Spiritual Promise
The Tao of Spirit
The Way Out Book
Walking with the Lord
Wealth & Higher Consciousness

For further information, please contact:
MSIA
P.O. Box 513935
Los Angeles, CA 90051-1935
323-737-4055
soul@msia.org
www.msia.org

LOVING EACH DAY

for

Moms & Dads

AN INSPIRATIONAL GUIDE
AND WORKING JOURNAL FOR PARENTS
TO ENRICH THE $\int$PIRIT WITHIN

JOHN-ROGER

MANDEVILLE PRESS
Los Angeles, California

Mandeville Press
P.O. Box 513935
Los Angeles, CA 90051-1935
323-737-4055
jrbooks@msia.org
www.mandevillepress.org

Printed in the United States of America
ISBN 1-893020-09-6

Introduction

E VERYONE knows you're supposed to love your children. Here's a book that, in simple, bottom line statements, tells how. It's amazing how a few words can get right to the heart of the matter, whether the topic is health, healthy relationships, homework, even sex education.

More than an information/how-to book for effective parenting, *Loving Each Day for Moms and Dads* is an inspirational guide. Its bite-sized pieces of insight have the power to move you to those "Aha!" solutions for raising happy, healthy, joyful children who can successfully navigate their way through life. Like the original *Loving Each Day*, this book is not to be stashed away on a bookshelf. Keep it by your bedside for a quick smile before sleep, keep it on the coffee table for instant inspiration, keep it in the kitchen or at your desk as a ready reference when challenges come up.

The pages are perforated so you can easily pull out the gems that particularly apply to your family and put them on the fridge, the bathroom mirror, your computer, your car dashboard, or copy them to send to friends as a constant source of upliftment.

A beautiful journal completes the book, with pages for you to record your experiences and awarenesses as your kids teach you the lessons of life. With sections guiding you through recording what makes you a great parent, how you can take care of yourself as a parent, how your child made you laugh today, evening time with your child, and much more, the journal is fun and supportive.

It has been said that insanity is hereditary; you get it from your kids. *Loving Each Day for Moms and Dads* can help bring you back to reality.

Every page is a reminder that there's nothing more important than the loving, each and every day.

 It is where the heart is that matters.

Trust is often one of the first things you see when you look into a child's eyes.

When children need something, they come to you to fulfill their prayers. They are depending on you to see what you can do to fulfill them. Don't be afraid to pick them up, cuddle them, love them, rub their backs and kiss and hug them. Give them all the love you can muster, and they will return it to you in more ways than you can imagine.

The early years of growing up are so important. When children are little, they must know that you're there, that you love them, that you care, that they can trust you, and that you're the one they can count on.

You don't have to earn love. If you let it, it will just flow from your children.

Do what you can to support yourself within the responsibilities that come with being a parent. Sometimes just fifteen or twenty minutes of quiet time daydreaming, meditating, or meandering in your own thoughts can be as refreshing as a cool shower on a hot day.

Children need love, and they need to be able to trust you. Don't let them down. Take good care of yourself so you have that good to offer your child.

Children learn best through love. When they love something, they look forward to it and are wide open to the information. When you prepare a loving place for children to come into, they can be open to receive the goodness you have in your heart for them.

Take the time to explain to your child what you are doing and why.

Explain to your kids that tests at school do not record their failure. Tests show areas where they can learn and grow, and point up their strengths. They are a reference point to know how they are doing, and to show them where to do more work.

Make your child's education an active one, where they are participating and learning by doing.

Children's games are make-believe. They're honest. Children have the flexibility to drop their games and go on to something else. It's a good thing for adults to do the same.

Give your children everything you have—with love. If you give just a little bit, you'll get weary. When you give your children everything you can, and support them totally, you'll be filled with the love of Spirit and the energy of that love as you go along.

Be honest with your children. If you lie to your child, you forfeit the greatest trust a child has.

Listen carefully to what your child is asking you, and respond to that level.

When you fight with your spouse or your children, you fight with the God within them. Sometimes you want to fight your loved one awake and say, "I see so much love in you, I just want to shake it loose!" Love them loose instead.

When your children come home from school, make sure that home is the playground, the paradise. Home represents the kingdom of heaven to children. It's the place to refuel and charge up their batteries.

Children are often brought together in a family to sandpaper each other and to teach each other. Your job is to see that no one gets hurt and that no one inflicts in an overpowering way against another. Other than that, your attitude can be that they will learn from one another.

Pressure can cause you to cry out, "For God's sake, leave me alone!" Then when the other person backs off, you may say, "No, wait… I didn't mean that." You just want them to give you a little space. You're really saying, "Just be tender, love me, let me breathe, let me feel that wonderful, free flowing loving inside of me."

Children who cry are not only crying for food and a change of diapers; they are also crying for love to be demonstrated to them. The nature of children is love. Love is natural to them—as it is to all of us.

If you feel like you can't say, "I love you," to your child or your spouse, go stand in front of a mirror and say, "I love you, I love you, I love you," until you break through that block. If you feel silly, stand in front of the mirror and say, "I'm silly, I'm silly, I'm silly," until you just don't care anymore. Don't let your emotions block you from honest, loving expression.

Love is part of your emotional structure, and you can use your love to help heal the world. You can certainly use it to bring healing to yourself and those close to you.

 With enough love, nothing is impossible.

If people close to you are not feeling well, do whatever you can to help them feel better. It's worth it. It can be a lot of fun if your attitude is in the right place.

Children are open to learning. Show them how things work. Let them *do* things. Give them some information, show them how to do it, then let them do it. Have them play the information back to you immediately. That's a test to see if they got it.

A friend was having trouble getting her son to do chores. She'd tried everything she could think of—no results. She sat him in the corner and he spit on the wall. She finally told him that when he did his chores by a certain time, he could have a popsicle. Close to that time, she took the popsicle out of the freezer and set it on the sink. If he got the chores done in time, he got the popsicle. If not, it melted. There were no second chances. Sometimes you have to be creative in your approach to discipline.

When you teach your children to face the world and the people in it with honesty and truth, you are giving them a most valuable key for living.

Take good care of yourself. Find out what works to fill you and balance you; then you can give of your overflow and loving to your family.

When you hide something, you are not being honest, and you will not have love. When you are open, saying, "You can see everything that is going on," then there is nothing hidden. All is present. That is very easy to live and to teach your children to live.

There is an innocence, openness, and trust in children that manifests as freedom.

A child communicates love by information, by talking about what's close to them, and one of the things closest to a child are the father and mother and what they do. The child will tell everyone about everything.

Kids teach each other to withstand the world. Their play teaches them how to win and lose, both inside and outside of themselves.

As long as your teen child/adult is doing no physical harm to him or herself or anyone else, you may as well see the humor in what they are doing and know that this, too, shall pass. In case you don't think so, just remember yourself, your attitudes, and your dress when you were a teen.

If a child loses a game and becomes so frustrated that they have a temper tantrum or withdraw and sulk, they may not be learning. When they can say, "It's just a game," and go on to the next thing, then they are learning.

When a child can let other children win, then they walk away winners, too. This is cooperation and flexibility.

Children need to learn to laugh at themselves and not to live their lives according to other people's opinions. Teach them to play roles and have fun with it. Let them dress up in funny costumes and have a good laugh at themselves. Let them put on plays and act out their ideas. They will learn important skills and gain self-confidence.

If one sister or brother is teasing another, teach the other child that he or she does not have to allow that. They can walk away from the situation and go somewhere else. We do this as adults. If we are in an irritating situation, we can ask others to change their approach. We can tell them we don't like their expression, and why. And if that doesn't work, we can either put up with it or leave. Teach your children the same choices.

Sometimes children let their imaginations run away with them, and you have screaming children on your hands for no apparent reason. Explain to them how the imagination works, that they create pictures and images, and that, if they want to, they can create happy pictures.

Play imagination games with your children. Show them how to imagine beautiful things, and how to change scary images into funny ones. If they see a monster chasing them, teach them to change that monster into a tiny monster and see it running off a cliff while they stand safely behind a tree and watch.

Help your children to envision their own success and happiness. If they have tests coming up in school, show them how to use their imaginations to see themselves taking the tests and passing them. Remember to make sure they study, too. Make it a game. Keep their attitude positive. Keep their spirits up and bright and active.

When you just love, with no restrictions, no qualifications, no conditions, you'll be so happy and joyful that you'll have a hard time containing it all. When you nurture this type of love in your home, that's the place you come to charge yourself so you can go back out in the world and do those things that must be done.

Teach your children that the rhythm of what they are doing can be their own rhythm when they are alone, and when they are with others, they must fit with the rhythm of the group. Then teach them harmony: not to be louder than others or off-key, how to blend with the group. Teach them to make their consciousness an addition to the group, not an irritation.

In teaching flexibility, you teach your children how to win and lose. When they really know how to lose a game gracefully, they'll be winners. Losing one game won't destroy their confidence or self-esteem. They'll handle it and go on to the next thing.

Teach your children to use what they can use and to allow other children to use what they can't. Let them play with a toy for as long as their interest holds, then show them how to exchange it for another. That helps them understand how not to get spread out too thin in the world or get involved with too many things at once.

Don't let your children "hoard" a lot of toys at the same time, because they can't play with them all at once. Let them learn to enjoy one thing at a time and move on to the next when they are ready.

Children can get spread out too thin very early in life. By the time they've finished sports, dance lessons, soccer, and band, they may be too tired to do their homework. Children need free time to just be children, too. Help them make choices so they enjoy and complete what they are doing, and feel good about themselves.

When you teach children, use their language to talk to them. If it's baby talk, you use baby-talk. If it's love-talk, you use love-talk. It should *all* be love-talk. Even when you are saying, "Shhh, be quiet," the child should not hear any harshness. The child should hear, "I love you very much; please be quiet now."

Let your children know that their work is their love in action. There are a lot of ways to demonstrate love. They can't always be hugging and kissing everyone to show their love. Show them that things like doing their homework and helping around the house are also demonstrations of their love.

Love your children equally when they are good and when they are bad—so that they know the love is always there.

If you are honest in giving your children sex education, in the timing that's right for them, you may be able to allow them to bypass sexual experience until they are ready to handle it emotionally and mentally. There are responsibilities and potential responsibilities on many levels that go with sexual intimacy, and children should be aware of these things.

When your child is misbehaving, you can help them by envisioning the positive. They will grasp the new image and move to that positive faster than you can imagine.

Raising a child isn't always easy, but it can be easier than we sometimes make it. If you relate to your child with loving consideration and respect, when that child gets to be sixteen, you probably won't have a problem on your hands. You're going to have a friend who will be a joy and a comfort.

Teach your children flexibility. Teach them how to move with what is going on, using games. They play one of your games, then you play one of theirs. Give them this idea of give and take.

If your kids are doing something that is irritating you, get in there and do it with them to some ridiculous extreme. Although you may have to go a long way, you'll help them complete what they were doing—for good. I did this one day with a young girl who was driving her mother up the wall playing with her food. I sat down with this little girl, and together we explored all the things you can do with your food. I showed her how to hold water in her mouth and let a little drool out one side of her mouth and then the other, how to suck the water back in through her teeth, and how to blow into her water glass. When I told her to take the water in her mouth and just let it drool all over her chin, neck, dress, and everything, she just quietly said, "No." That was the end of it. It was pretty sloppy, but it was over in a half-hour instead of weeks of frustration for her Mom. This technique can be effective in certain areas.

When you are setting up household chores for your children, make sure they know what to do physically. Show them how to do it, and do it with them a time or two. Make it fun.

An important element of discipline is *love*. When you discipline your child, do it out of love, not out of your lack or anger or frustration.

Hold your children to their responsibilities and teach them how to get along more effectively with themselves and others out of your love and concern for your child.

Appearing human or imperfect in front of your children is wonderful. When your child sees that Mom and Dad go through rough times, too, they'll feel more freedom to be themselves. They'll know they are still worthy of your love even when they make a mistake.

It's okay to apologize to your children. You can make mistakes, too. They'll still love you.

If you feel badly after you discipline your child, you probably over-disciplined them or disciplined out of your anger rather than out of your love. When you discipline out of your anger and frustration, you are disciplining the wrong person. Take some time with yourself.

After you set boundaries for your children's behavior and wellbeing, you must keep the boundaries for the children until they can keep them for themselves. If you don't keep them consistent, they will find no value in them.

Help your child explore the house. Let them take everything out of the linen closet, and then show them how to fold it up and put it all back. If it's not done perfectly, who cares? You can put the towels back correctly next time you use them.

Children are trying to learn about this world as fast as they can. If you help them in their learning, you'll be much further ahead, and so will they.

When kids feel they are not getting the love and attention to which they're entitled, they may go to all sorts of extremes to get what they want. One way is a temper tantrum. A way to stop children from throwing a tantrum is to get down on the floor with them and do it as loud or louder. They'll see what they look like and it will sort of embarrass them. If they realize you're doing it because they're doing it, they'll stay out of that area. This technique can bring results in other areas, too.

Don't wish that your children be just like you; wish that they fulfill their own destiny in the best way possible. And wish that, rather than blocking them, you have the wit to assist them.

When your children ask you questions, give them honest answers. Don't put them off with excuses or lies or anything else. Take the time to educate them and explain this world to them.

Society is so full of educational information that if you think you can tell your kids the facts of life when they are fourteen, you'll be way too late.

Children do not have to learn about sexual things through experience. You can teach them a lot through open, honest discussion. Let them ask questions and tell you what's on their minds; nurture communication with your children.

If you go into shock when your child uses a word that you think is "nasty," go stand in front of the mirror and say that word over and over until it loses its power over you. Then you'll be able to direct your child into better expressions, rather than reacting when he or she says something "dirty."

If your children are determined to have their own way, choose an area that won't do any harm and let them have their way, totally, in that area. Let your baby pull out all the pots and pans from the cupboard. The baby will learn what they are. Then he or she also gets to help put them all back—and that's important, too.

Instead of telling your child, "Go clean up your room so Mommy will love you," or "Clean up your room so Daddy will be proud of you," tell them, "Clean up your room because I want you to." That's honest, and it's reasonable.

We're vital, alive human beings, and part of our existence here is loving, caring, and sharing. Cultivate what works *for* you in every area —emotionally, financially, physically—all of it. Take good care of yourself. Then you can give from the overflow of your loving and abundance.

Don't make it a federal crime if a child messes up. If the child makes errors, in school or at home, understand that making errors is part of learning. If a child were born perfect, you wouldn't be needed.

If you have children, make sure you care enough for yourself, your spouse, and your children to balance your life.

When a child is born into a family, the adults must make substantial adjustments. Love and support each other as lovers, and appreciate your roles as mother and father. Loving and supporting your child is easy then, and adds to your life as you all nurture one another.

Let your child know that it is okay to make mistakes, from missing a question on a test to spilling their milk. When you make it all right to do well *and* to make mistakes, your child will probably not lie to you.

Your child is just beginning to grow and learn, and believe it or not, you are not finished with your learning either. You can learn on both the inner and outer levels all your life.

When you don't have to, don't be in charge. As long as it does not endanger the child or break an arrangement on which you two agreed, give your children freedom to express themselves even when their expression is different from yours.

There will be times when you ask your child to do something and they make it clear that your idea is not their choice. If you start to get impatient or irritable, ask yourself, "Do I want my child to do this because of my will or ego, or because it's necessary?"

If you develop the habit of telling your child the truth no matter what, your child is likely to treat you the same way.

You can love your children and still need time to be alone or with other adults. You can form a community of friends with similar interests and find ways to support each other. It isn't always easy, but it's worth it.

During this process of raising your child, remember to touch. A hug, a pat, a squeeze, a stroke—all those loving, physical expressions are recorded in the child's heart forever.

Love your children and yourself enough not to put up with anything less than the truth—from yourself or from them. They may not like it initially, but in time they will respect your allegiance to the truth.

Some teenagers are into drugs or alcohol. Be careful not to hold an attitude of judge and jury ready to sentence your child to a life without your loving. What they need is your corrective guidance, loving, and acceptance; they need to know that you care. You may have to be the "benevolent dictator," but don't withdraw your love.

Do you want your child to grow up to be a nurturing, caring, supportive human being? Children learn though imitation.

Give yourself time to get in touch with you. With no judgments and with compassion, take the time to review events, thoughts, and feelings; then take the time to read what's written in your heart.

Raising a child can bring everything from fulfillment to boredom, from being a loving support to being a maid, from rapture to the ridiculous. That's all part of the deal.

Wise couples take time together, away from their children. This is not a crass, selfish action; parents need to renew their adult bonding with each other. That loving is the strength and foundation that the child can depend on.

As the family is strong in its nature, the community gets strong. As society gets strong, culture and civilization grow, and spirituality moves in. It is on *love* that all this is built.

See if there are some areas where you can lighten up. One of the best ways to relieve tension is with humor. It's never too late to have a happy childhood.

On Being a Parent

Journal

What makes me a great parent:

_____

_____

_____

_____

_____

_____

_____

_____

_____

_____

_____

_____

_____

_____

_____

_____

_____

_____

_____

_____

_____

_____

On Being a Parent

Journal

What makes me a great parent:

_____

_____

_____

_____

_____

_____

_____

_____

_____

_____

_____

_____

_____

_____

_____

_____

_____

_____

_____

_____

_____

_____

_____

ON BEING A PARENT

What makes me a great parent:

_____

_____

_____

_____

_____

_____

_____

_____

_____

_____

_____

_____

_____

_____

_____

_____

_____

_____

_____

_____

_____

ON BEING A PARENT

Journal

What makes me a great parent:

_____

_____

_____

_____

_____

_____

_____

_____

_____

_____

_____

_____

_____

_____

_____

_____

_____

_____

_____

_____

ON BEING A PARENT

Journal

What makes me a great parent:

_____

_____

_____

_____

_____

_____

_____

_____

_____

_____

_____

_____

_____

_____

_____

_____

_____

_____

_____

_____

_____

_____

_____

_____

ON BEING A PARENT

My best parenting strengths are:

_____

_____

_____

_____

_____

_____

_____

_____

_____

_____

_____

_____

_____

_____

_____

_____

_____

_____

_____

_____

_____

ON BEING A PARENT

Journal

My best parenting strengths are:

_____

_____

_____

_____

_____

_____

_____

_____

_____

_____

_____

_____

_____

_____

_____

_____

_____

_____

_____

_____

_____

On Being a Parent

My best parenting strengths are:

_____

_____

_____

_____

_____

_____

_____

_____

_____

_____

_____

_____

_____

_____

_____

_____

_____

_____

_____

_____

_____

On Being a Parent

Journal

My best parenting strengths are:

_____

_____

_____

_____

_____

_____

_____

_____

_____

_____

_____

_____

_____

_____

_____

_____

_____

_____

_____

_____

_____

On Being a Parent

My best parenting strengths are:

_____

_____

_____

_____

_____

_____

_____

_____

_____

_____

_____

_____

_____

_____

_____

_____

_____

_____

_____

_____

On Being a Parent

My best parenting strengths are:

_____

_____

_____

_____

_____

_____

_____

_____

_____

_____

_____

_____

_____

_____

_____

_____

_____

_____

_____

_____

_____

Journal

Ways that I can take care of myself:

_____

_____

_____

_____

_____

_____

_____

_____

_____

_____

_____

_____

_____

_____

_____

_____

_____

_____

_____

_____

_____

Ways that I can take care of myself:

_____

_____

_____

_____

_____

_____

_____

_____

_____

_____

_____

_____

_____

_____

_____

_____

_____

_____

_____

_____

ON BEING A PARENT

Journal

Ways that I can take care of myself:

_____

_____

_____

_____

_____

_____

_____

_____

_____

_____

_____

_____

_____

_____

_____

_____

_____

_____

_____

_____

Ways that I can take care of myself:

_____

_____

_____

_____

_____

_____

_____

_____

_____

_____

_____

_____

_____

_____

_____

_____

_____

_____

_____

_____

On Being a Parent

Ways that I expressed my loving for
my husband or wife today:

_____

_____

_____

_____

_____

_____

_____

_____

_____

_____

_____

_____

_____

_____

_____

_____

_____

_____

_____

ON BEING A PARENT

Journal

Ways that I expressed my loving for
my husband or wife today:

_____

_____

_____

_____

_____

_____

_____

_____

_____

_____

_____

_____

_____

_____

_____

_____

_____

_____

_____

_____

ON BEING A PARENT

Journal

Ways that I expressed my loving for
my husband or wife today:

_____

_____

_____

_____

_____

_____

_____

_____

_____

_____

_____

_____

_____

_____

_____

_____

_____

_____

_____

Journal

Ways that I expressed my loving for
my husband or wife today:

_____

_____

_____

_____

_____

_____

_____

_____

_____

_____

_____

_____

_____

_____

_____

_____

_____

_____

_____

_____

_____

_____

ON BEING A PARENT

Journal

Ways that I expressed my loving for
my child today:

_____

_____

_____

_____

_____

_____

_____

_____

_____

_____

_____

_____

_____

_____

_____

_____

_____

_____

_____

_____

_____

ON BEING A PARENT

Journal

Ways that I expressed my loving for
my child today:

_____

_____

_____

_____

_____

_____

_____

_____

_____

_____

_____

_____

_____

_____

_____

_____

_____

_____

_____

_____

_____

_____

ON BEING A PARENT

Ways that I expressed my loving for
my child today:

_____

_____

_____

_____

_____

_____

_____

_____

_____

_____

_____

_____

_____

_____

_____

_____

_____

_____

_____

ON BEING A PARENT

Journal

Ways that I expressed my loving for
my child today:

_____

_____

_____

_____

_____

_____

_____

_____

_____

_____

_____

_____

_____

_____

_____

_____

_____

_____

_____

_____

_____

ON BEING A PARENT

Journal

What I appreciate about myself
as a parent today:

_____

_____

_____

_____

_____

_____

_____

_____

_____

_____

_____

_____

_____

_____

_____

_____

_____

_____

_____

_____

_____

ON BEING A PARENT

What I appreciate about myself
as a parent today:

_____

_____

_____

_____

_____

_____

_____

_____

_____

_____

_____

_____

_____

_____

_____

_____

_____

_____

_____

On Being a Parent

What I appreciate about myself
as a parent today:

_____

_____

_____

_____

_____

_____

_____

_____

_____

_____

_____

_____

_____

_____

_____

_____

_____

_____

_____

_____

_____

_____

_____

ON BEING A PARENT

Journal

What I appreciate about myself
as a parent today:

_____

_____

_____

_____

_____

_____

_____

_____

_____

_____

_____

_____

_____

_____

_____

_____

_____

_____

_____

_____

ON BEING A PARENT

What I'd like to do better as a
parent tomorrow:

_____

_____

_____

_____

_____

_____

_____

_____

_____

_____

_____

_____

_____

_____

_____

_____

_____

_____

_____

_____

_____

_____

_____

ON BEING A PARENT

Journal

What I'd like to do better as a
parent tomorrow:

_____

_____

_____

_____

_____

_____

_____

_____

_____

_____

_____

_____

_____

_____

_____

_____

_____

_____

_____

_____

ON BEING A PARENT

What I'd like to do better as a
parent tomorrow:

_____

_____

_____

_____

_____

_____

_____

_____

_____

_____

_____

_____

_____

_____

_____

_____

_____

_____

_____

_____

_____

_____

ON BEING A PARENT

Journal

What I'd like to do better as a
parent tomorrow:

_____

_____

_____

_____

_____

_____

_____

_____

_____

_____

_____

_____

_____

_____

_____

_____

_____

_____

_____

_____

ON BEING A PARENT

Journal

What I enjoyed about being a
parent today:

_____

_____

_____

_____

_____

_____

_____

_____

_____

_____

_____

_____

_____

_____

_____

_____

_____

_____

_____

_____

_____

_____

ON BEING A PARENT

What I enjoyed about being a
parent today:

_____

_____

_____

_____

_____

_____

_____

_____

_____

_____

_____

_____

_____

_____

_____

_____

_____

_____

_____

_____

_____

_____

ON BEING A PARENT

Journal

What I enjoyed about being a
parent today:

_____

_____

_____

_____

_____

_____

_____

_____

_____

_____

_____

_____

_____

_____

_____

_____

_____

_____

_____

_____

_____

_____

ON BEING A PARENT

Journal

What I enjoyed about being a
parent today:

_____

_____

_____

_____

_____

_____

_____

_____

_____

_____

_____

_____

_____

_____

_____

_____

_____

_____

_____

_____

_____

ON BEING A PARENT

Journal

The blessing I am to my child:

_____

_____

_____

_____

_____

_____

_____

_____

_____

_____

_____

_____

_____

_____

_____

_____

_____

_____

_____

_____

_____

_____

_____

ON BEING A PARENT

Journal

The blessing I am to my child:

_____

_____

_____

_____

_____

_____

_____

_____

_____

_____

_____

_____

_____

_____

_____

_____

_____

_____

_____

_____

_____

_____

_____

The blessing I am to my child:

_____

_____

_____

_____

_____

_____

_____

_____

_____

_____

_____

_____

_____

_____

_____

_____

_____

_____

_____

_____

_____

_____

_____

ON BEING A PARENT

The blessing I am to my child:

_____

_____

_____

_____

_____

_____

_____

_____

_____

_____

_____

_____

_____

_____

_____

_____

_____

_____

_____

ON BEING A PARENT

The blessing I am to my child:

_____

_____

_____

_____

_____

_____

_____

_____

_____

_____

_____

_____

_____

_____

_____

_____

_____

_____

_____

_____

Choose a Quote from the Book

Journal

What my child thinks about this quote:

_____

_____

_____

_____

_____

_____

_____

_____

_____

_____

_____

_____

_____

_____

_____

_____

_____

_____

_____

_____

_____

_____

_____

CHOOSE A QUOTE FROM THE BOOK

Journal

What I think about this quote:

_____

_____

_____

_____

_____

_____

_____

_____

_____

_____

_____

_____

_____

_____

_____

_____

_____

_____

_____

_____

CHOOSE A QUOTE FROM THE BOOK

Journal

What my husband or wife thinks
about this quote:

_____

_____

_____

_____

_____

_____

_____

_____

_____

_____

_____

_____

_____

_____

_____

_____

_____

_____

_____

_____

_____

_____

CHOOSE A QUOTE FROM THE BOOK

Journal

What my child thinks about this quote:

_____

_____

_____

_____

_____

_____

_____

_____

_____

_____

_____

_____

_____

_____

_____

_____

_____

_____

_____

_____

_____

_____

CHOOSE A QUOTE FROM THE BOOK

Journal

What I think about this quote:

_____

_____

_____

_____

_____

_____

_____

_____

_____

_____

_____

_____

_____

_____

_____

_____

_____

_____

_____

_____

_____

CHOOSE A QUOTE FROM THE BOOK

Journal

What my husband or wife thinks
about this quote:

_____

_____

_____

_____

_____

_____

_____

_____

_____

_____

_____

_____

_____

_____

_____

_____

_____

_____

_____

_____

_____

CHOOSE A QUOTE FROM THE BOOK

What my child thinks about this quote:

_____

_____

_____

_____

_____

_____

_____

_____

_____

_____

_____

_____

_____

_____

_____

_____

_____

_____

_____

_____

_____

_____

CHOOSE A QUOTE FROM THE BOOK

Journal

What I think about this quote:

_____

_____

_____

_____

_____

_____

_____

_____

_____

_____

_____

_____

_____

_____

_____

_____

_____

_____

_____

_____

CHOOSE A QUOTE FROM THE BOOK

Journal

What my husband or wife thinks
about this quote:

_____

_____

_____

_____

_____

_____

_____

_____

_____

_____

_____

_____

_____

_____

_____

_____

_____

_____

_____

_____

_____

_____

CHOOSE A QUOTE FROM THE BOOK

Journal

What my child thinks about this quote:

_____

_____

_____

_____

_____

_____

_____

_____

_____

_____

_____

_____

_____

_____

_____

_____

_____

_____

_____

_____

_____

CHOOSE A QUOTE FROM THE BOOK

Journal

What I think about this quote:

_____

_____

_____

_____

_____

_____

_____

_____

_____

_____

_____

_____

_____

_____

_____

_____

_____

_____

_____

_____

_____

_____

CHOOSE A QUOTE FROM THE BOOK

Journal

What my husband or wife thinks
about this quote:

_____

_____

_____

_____

_____

_____

_____

_____

_____

_____

_____

_____

_____

_____

_____

_____

_____

_____

_____

What my child revealed to me today:

_____

_____

_____

_____

_____

_____

_____

_____

_____

_____

_____

_____

_____

_____

_____

_____

_____

_____

_____

_____

What my child revealed to me today:

_____

_____

_____

_____

_____

_____

_____

_____

_____

_____

_____

_____

_____

_____

_____

_____

_____

_____

_____

_____

_____

ON LEARNING

What my child revealed to me today:

_____

_____

_____

_____

_____

_____

_____

_____

_____

_____

_____

_____

_____

_____

_____

_____

_____

_____

_____

_____

_____

_____

ON LEARNING

Journal

What my child revealed to me today:

_____

_____

_____

_____

_____

_____

_____

_____

_____

_____

_____

_____

_____

_____

_____

_____

_____

_____

_____

_____

_____

ON LEARNING

What my child revealed to me today:

_____

_____

_____

_____

_____

_____

_____

_____

_____

_____

_____

_____

_____

_____

_____

_____

_____

_____

_____

_____

ON LEARNING

What I revealed to myself today:

_____

_____

_____

_____

_____

_____

_____

_____

_____

_____

_____

_____

_____

_____

_____

_____

_____

_____

_____

ON LEARNING

What I revealed to myself today:

_____

_____

_____

_____

_____

_____

_____

_____

_____

_____

_____

_____

_____

_____

_____

_____

_____

_____

_____

_____

ON LEARNING

Journal

What I revealed to myself today:

_____

_____

_____

_____

_____

_____

_____

_____

_____

_____

_____

_____

_____

_____

_____

_____

_____

_____

_____

_____

_____

_____

_____

ON LEARNING

Journal

What I revealed to myself today:

_____

_____

_____

_____

_____

_____

_____

_____

_____

_____

_____

_____

_____

_____

_____

_____

_____

_____

_____

_____

ON LEARNING

Journal

What I revealed to myself today:

_____

_____

_____

_____

_____

_____

_____

_____

_____

_____

_____

_____

_____

_____

_____

_____

_____

_____

_____

_____

_____

_____

ON LEARNING

Journal

What I revealed to myself today:

_____

_____

_____

_____

_____

_____

_____

_____

_____

_____

_____

_____

_____

_____

_____

_____

_____

_____

_____

_____

_____

_____

ON LEARNING

Journal

What my child learned today:

_____

_____

_____

_____

_____

_____

_____

_____

_____

_____

_____

_____

_____

_____

_____

_____

_____

_____

_____

_____

_____

_____

_____

On Learning

Journal

What my child learned today:

_____

_____

_____

_____

_____

_____

_____

_____

_____

_____

_____

_____

_____

_____

_____

_____

_____

_____

_____

_____

On Learning

What my child learned today:

_____

_____

_____

_____

_____

_____

_____

_____

_____

_____

_____

_____

_____

_____

_____

_____

_____

_____

_____

_____

_____

_____

ON LEARNING

What my child learned today:

_____

_____

_____

_____

_____

_____

_____

_____

_____

_____

_____

_____

_____

_____

_____

_____

_____

_____

_____

_____

_____

On Learning

Journal

What my child learned today:

_____

_____

_____

_____

_____

_____

_____

_____

_____

_____

_____

_____

_____

_____

_____

_____

_____

_____

_____

_____

_____

ON LEARNING

Journal

What my child learned today:

_____

_____

_____

_____

_____

_____

_____

_____

_____

_____

_____

_____

_____

_____

_____

_____

_____

_____

_____

_____

_____

_____

_____

ON LEARNING

What I learned today as a parent:

_____

_____

_____

_____

_____

_____

_____

_____

_____

_____

_____

_____

_____

_____

_____

_____

_____

_____

_____

_____

_____

_____

ON LEARNING

Journal

What I learned today as a parent:

_____

_____

_____

_____

_____

_____

_____

_____

_____

_____

_____

_____

_____

_____

_____

_____

_____

_____

_____

_____

_____

ON LEARNING

What I learned today as a parent:

_____

_____

_____

_____

_____

_____

_____

_____

_____

_____

_____

_____

_____

_____

_____

_____

_____

_____

_____

_____

_____

Journal

What I learned today as a parent:

_____

_____

_____

_____

_____

_____

_____

_____

_____

_____

_____

_____

_____

_____

_____

_____

_____

_____

_____

_____

_____

On Learning

What I learned today as a parent:

_____

_____

_____

_____

_____

_____

_____

_____

_____

_____

_____

_____

_____

_____

_____

_____

_____

_____

_____

_____

_____

ON LEARNING

What I learned today as a parent:

_____

_____

_____

_____

_____

_____

_____

_____

_____

_____

_____

_____

_____

_____

_____

_____

_____

_____

_____

EVENING TIME WITH MY CHILD

Journal

What my child liked about today that he or she
would like to do again tomorrow:

_____

_____

_____

_____

_____

_____

_____

_____

_____

_____

_____

_____

_____

_____

_____

_____

_____

_____

_____

_____

_____

_____

EVENING TIME WITH MY CHILD

Journal

What my child didn't like about today that she or
he would not like to do again tomorrow:

EVENING TIME WITH MY CHILD

What would my child like to do differently
tomorrow from what s/he did today?

_____

_____

_____

_____

_____

_____

_____

_____

_____

_____

_____

_____

_____

_____

_____

_____

_____

_____

_____

_____

Evening Time with my Child

What my child liked about today that he or she
would like to do again tomorrow:

_____

_____

_____

_____

_____

_____

_____

_____

_____

_____

_____

_____

_____

_____

_____

_____

_____

_____

_____

EVENING TIME WITH MY CHILD

Journal

What my child didn't like about today that she or
he would not like to do again tomorrow:

_____

_____

_____

_____

_____

_____

_____

_____

_____

_____

_____

_____

_____

_____

_____

_____

_____

_____

_____

_____

EVENING TIME WITH MY CHILD

Journal

What would my child like to do differently
tomorrow from what s/he did today?

_____

_____

_____

_____

_____

_____

_____

_____

_____

_____

_____

_____

_____

_____

_____

_____

_____

_____

_____

_____

_____

EVENING TIME WITH MY CHILD

Journal

What my child liked about today that he or she
would like to do again tomorrow:

_____

_____

_____

_____

_____

_____

_____

_____

_____

_____

_____

_____

_____

_____

_____

_____

_____

_____

_____

_____

_____

_____

_____

EVENING TIME WITH MY CHILD

Journal

What my child didn't like about today that she or
he would not like to do again tomorrow:

_____

_____

_____

_____

_____

_____

_____

_____

_____

_____

_____

_____

_____

_____

_____

_____

_____

_____

_____

_____

_____

_____

What would my child like to do differently
tomorrow from what s/he did today?

_____

_____

_____

_____

_____

_____

_____

_____

_____

_____

_____

_____

_____

_____

_____

_____

_____

_____

_____

_____

Journal

What my child liked about today that he or she
would like to do again tomorrow:

_____

_____

_____

_____

_____

_____

_____

_____

_____

_____

_____

_____

_____

_____

_____

_____

_____

_____

_____

_____

_____

_____

_____

_____

EVENING TIME WITH MY CHILD

Journal

What my child didn't like about today that she or
he would not like to do again tomorrow:

_____

_____

_____

_____

_____

_____

_____

_____

_____

_____

_____

_____

_____

_____

_____

_____

_____

_____

_____

_____

What would my child like to do differently
tomorrow from what s/he did today?

_____

_____

_____

_____

_____

_____

_____

_____

_____

_____

_____

_____

_____

_____

_____

_____

_____

_____

_____

_____

EVENING TIME WITH MY CHILD

Journal

What my child liked about today that he or she would like to do again tomorrow:

_____

_____

_____

_____

_____

_____

_____

_____

_____

_____

_____

_____

_____

_____

_____

_____

_____

_____

_____

_____

EVENING TIME WITH MY CHILD

Journal

What my child didn't like about today that she or
he would not like to do again tomorrow:

_____

_____

_____

_____

_____

_____

_____

_____

_____

_____

_____

_____

_____

_____

_____

_____

_____

_____

_____

_____

_____

_____

Journal

What would my child like to do differently
tomorrow from what s/he did today?

_____

_____

_____

_____

_____

_____

_____

_____

_____

_____

_____

_____

_____

_____

_____

_____

_____

_____

_____

_____

_____

_____

_____

EVENING TIME WITH MY CHILD

Journal

What my child liked about today that he or she
would like to do again tomorrow:

_____

_____

_____

_____

_____

_____

_____

_____

_____

_____

_____

_____

_____

_____

_____

_____

_____

_____

_____

_____

_____

EVENING TIME WITH MY CHILD

Journal

What my child didn't like about today that she or
he would not like to do again tomorrow:

_____

_____

_____

_____

_____

_____

_____

_____

_____

_____

_____

_____

_____

_____

_____

_____

_____

_____

_____

_____

_____

_____

_____

Evening Time with My Child

Journal

What would my child like to do differently
tomorrow from what s/he did today?

_____

_____

_____

_____

_____

_____

_____

_____

_____

_____

_____

_____

_____

_____

_____

_____

_____

_____

_____

_____

_____

EVENING TIME WITH MY CHILD

Journal

What my child liked about today that he or she
would like to do again tomorrow:

_____

_____

_____

_____

_____

_____

_____

_____

_____

_____

_____

_____

_____

_____

_____

_____

_____

_____

_____

EVENING TIME WITH MY CHILD

Journal

What my child didn't like about today that she or
he would not like to do again tomorrow:

_____

_____

_____

_____

_____

_____

_____

_____

_____

_____

_____

_____

_____

_____

_____

_____

_____

_____

EVENING TIME WITH MY CHILD

Journal

What would my child like to do differently
tomorrow from what s/he did today?

_____

_____

_____

_____

_____

_____

_____

_____

_____

_____

_____

_____

_____

_____

_____

_____

_____

_____

_____

_____

_____

EVENING TIME WITH MY CHILD

Journal

What my child liked about today that he or she
would like to do again tomorrow:

_____

_____

_____

_____

_____

_____

_____

_____

_____

_____

_____

_____

_____

_____

_____

_____

_____

_____

_____

_____

EVENING TIME WITH MY CHILD

Journal

What my child didn't like about today that she or he would not like to do again tomorrow:

_____

_____

_____

_____

_____

_____

_____

_____

_____

_____

_____

_____

_____

_____

_____

_____

_____

_____

_____

_____

What would my child like to do differently
tomorrow from what s/he did today?

_____

_____

_____

_____

_____

_____

_____

_____

_____

_____

_____

_____

_____

_____

_____

_____

_____

_____

_____

_____

_____

EVENING TIME WITH MY CHILD

Journal

What my child liked about today that he or she would like to do again tomorrow:

_____

_____

_____

_____

_____

_____

_____

_____

_____

_____

_____

_____

_____

_____

_____

_____

_____

_____

_____

What my child didn't like about today that she or he would not like to do again tomorrow:

_____

_____

_____

_____

_____

_____

_____

_____

_____

_____

_____

_____

_____

_____

_____

_____

_____

_____

_____

_____

_____

EVENING TIME WITH MY CHILD

Journal

What would my child like to do differently
tomorrow from what s/he did today?

_____

_____

_____

_____

_____

_____

_____

_____

_____

_____

_____

_____

_____

_____

_____

_____

_____

_____

_____

_____

How my child made me laugh today:

_____

_____

_____

_____

_____

_____

_____

_____

_____

_____

_____

_____

_____

_____

_____

_____

_____

_____

_____

_____

How my child made me laugh today:

_____

_____

_____

_____

_____

_____

_____

_____

_____

_____

_____

_____

_____

_____

_____

_____

_____

_____

_____

_____

Journal

How my child made me laugh today:

_____

_____

_____

_____

_____

_____

_____

_____

_____

_____

_____

_____

_____

_____

_____

_____

_____

_____

_____

SPECIAL MOMENTS

Journal

How my child made me laugh today:

_____

_____

_____

_____

_____

_____

_____

_____

_____

_____

_____

_____

_____

_____

_____

_____

_____

_____

_____

_____

SPECIAL MOMENTS

Journal

What my child said today:

_____

_____

_____

_____

_____

_____

_____

_____

_____

_____

_____

_____

_____

_____

_____

_____

_____

_____

_____

_____

SPECIAL MOMENTS

Journal

What my child said today:

_____

_____

_____

_____

_____

_____

_____

_____

_____

_____

_____

_____

_____

_____

_____

_____

_____

_____

_____

_____

SPECIAL MOMENTS

Journal

What my child said today:

_____

_____

_____

_____

_____

_____

_____

_____

_____

_____

_____

_____

_____

_____

_____

_____

_____

_____

_____

_____

SPECIAL MOMENTS

Journal

What my child said today:

_____

_____

_____

_____

_____

_____

_____

_____

_____

_____

_____

_____

_____

_____

_____

_____

_____

_____

_____

_____

_____

Journal

What my child said today:

_____

_____

_____

_____

_____

_____

_____

_____

_____

_____

_____

_____

_____

_____

_____

_____

_____

_____

_____

_____

_____

_____

_____

_____

_____

SPECIAL MOMENTS

Journal

What my child said today:

_____

_____

_____

_____

_____

_____

_____

_____

_____

_____

_____

_____

_____

_____

_____

_____

_____

_____

_____

_____

_____

_____

SPECIAL MOMENTS

Journal

What my child did today:

_____

_____

_____

_____

_____

_____

_____

_____

_____

_____

_____

_____

_____

_____

_____

_____

_____

_____

_____

_____

_____

_____

SPECIAL MOMENTS

Journal

What my child did today:

_____

_____

_____

_____

_____

_____

_____

_____

_____

_____

_____

_____

_____

_____

_____

_____

_____

_____

_____

_____

_____

_____

SPECIAL MOMENTS

Journal

What my child did today:

_____

_____

_____

_____

_____

_____

_____

_____

_____

_____

_____

_____

_____

_____

_____

_____

_____

_____

_____

_____

Journal

What my child did today:

_____

_____

_____

_____

_____

_____

_____

_____

_____

_____

_____

_____

_____

_____

_____

_____

_____

_____

_____

_____

_____

_____

_____

SPECIAL MOMENTS

Journal

What my child did today:

_____

_____

_____

_____

_____

_____

_____

_____

_____

_____

_____

_____

_____

_____

_____

_____

_____

_____

_____

_____

_____

_____

_____

ABOUT THE AUTHOR

A TEACHER AND LECTURER of international stature, with millions of books in print, John-Roger is a luminary in the lives of many people around the world. For over three decades, his wisdom, humor, common sense and love have helped people to discover the Spirit within themselves and find health, peace, and prosperity.

With two co-authored books on the *New York Times* Bestseller List to his credit, and more than three dozen self-help books and audio albums, John-Roger offers extraordinary insights on a wide range of topics.

He is the founder of the nondenominational Church of the Movement of Spiritual Inner Awareness (MSIA) which focuses on Soul Transcendence; Chancellor of the University of Santa Monica; President of Peace Theological Seminary & College of Philosophy; and founder of Insight Transformational Seminars.

John-Roger has given over 5,000 lectures and seminars worldwide, many of which are televised nationally on his cable program, "That Which Is," through the Network of Wisdoms. He has been a featured guest on "Larry King Live," "Politically Incorrect," "The Roseane Show," and appears regularly on radio and television.

An educator and minister by profession, John-Roger continues to transform lives by educating people in the wisdom of the spiritual heart.

If you have enjoyed this book, you may want to explore the following resources through the Movement of Spiritual Inner Awareness, where John-Roger serves as Spiritual Advisor:

Loving Each Day Subscription

Loving Each Day quotes are offered in the form of a daily e-mail message from MSIA that contains an uplifting quote or passage from John-Roger or John Morton, MSIA's Spiritual Director. Intended to inspire and support, the quotes assist you to reflect on the Spirit within. *Loving Each Day* is available in four languages–English, Spanish, French and Portuguese.

A subscription is free upon request.

To subscribe, please visit the web site, www.msia.org.

Loving Each Day

by John-Roger

Loving Each Day is a book of daily meditations to assist you in focusing on and discovering more of the wisdom, truth, and beauty within. A simple approach to tapping the abundance of the Spirit within.

$18, hardbound

ISBN 0-914829-26-2

Available in bookstores everywhere

or from MSIA at 323-737-4055,

www.msia.org

Relationships: Love, Marriage and Spirit
by John-Roger

Relationships offer us some of our greatest challenges and we often look to them for our deepest satisfaction. John-Roger recognizes the stumbling blocks to successful relationships, and offers insight and practical tools to nurturing, loving, sharing, happiness and fulfillment.

$20, hardbound

ISBN 1-893020-05-3

Available in bookstores everywhere

or from MSIA at 323-737-4055

www.msia.org